Please listen, subscribe, and review the *Social Selling Made Simple* podcast, http://socialsellingmadesimplepodcast.com.

Social Selling Made Simple is the place for real estate professionals to learn how to use social media and tech, so you can sell more homes and help more people.

The Modern Real Estate Professionals Guide to Success

Building a Sustainable and Successful Real Estate Business in Today's World

Marki Lemons Ryhal

THiNK*aha*®

An Actionable Business Journal

E-mail: info@thinkaha.com
20660 Stevens Creek Blvd., Suite 210
Cupertino, CA 95014

Copyright © 2019, Marki Lemons Ryhal

Please go to
http://aha.pub/RealEstateGuide
to read this AHAbook and to share the
individual AHAmessages that resonate with you.

Published by THiNKaha®
20660 Stevens Creek Blvd., Suite 210,
Cupertino, CA 95014
http://thinkaha.com
E-mail: **info@thinkaha.com**

First Printing: November 2019
Hardcover ISBN: 978-1-61699-340-5   1-61699-340-5
Paperback ISBN: 978-1-61699-339-9   1-61699-339-1
eBook ISBN: 978-1-61699-341-2   1-61699-341-3
Place of Publication: Silicon Valley, California, USA
Paperback Library of Congress Number: 2019911617

Trademarks

Warning and Disclaimer

Dedication

This book is dedicated to the three men who hold the keys to my heart—Austin, Skyler, and Stephen. I love each of you with every ounce of my being. You are my WHY!

This book is also in loving memory of my mother, Hazel Denise Lemons.

How to Read a THiNKaha® Book
A Note from the Publisher

The AHAthat/THiNKaha series is the CliffsNotes of the 21st century. These books are contextual in nature. Although the actual words won't change, their meaning will every time you read one as your context will change. Be ready, you will experience your own AHA moments as you read the AHA messages™ in this book. They are designed to be stand-alone actionable messages that will help you think about a project you're working on, an event, a sales deal, a personal issue, etc., differently. As you read this book, please think about the following:

1. It should only take 15–20 minutes to read this book the first time out. When you're reading, write in the underlined area one to three action items that resonate with you.
2. Mark your calendar to re-read this book again in 30 days.
3. Repeat step #1 and mark one to three more AHA messages that resonate. They will most likely be different than the first time. BTW: this is also a great time to reflect on the AHA messages that resonated with you during your last reading.

After reading a THiNKaha book, marking your AHA messages, re-reading it, and marking more AHA messages, you'll begin to see how these books contextually apply to you. AHAthat/THiNKaha books advocate for continuous, lifelong learning. They will help you transform your AHAs into actionable items with tangible results until you no longer have to say AHA to these moments—they'll become part of your daily practice as you continue to grow and learn.

Mitchell Levy, The AHA Guy at AHAthat
publisher@thinkaha.com

THiNKaha®

Contents

Preface

Marki Lemons Ryhal always finds a way to get it done. In 2006, Marki lost it all. Her grandfather passed away from Alzheimer's disease; her mother passed away two months later from a brain aneurysm; and then Marki found out that she had a high-risk pregnancy at age thirty-six, and she fainted on an airplane. In the midst of losing everything except her mind, she vividly remembered the 2006 REALTORS® Profile of Buyers and Sellers, and as a result, she decided to embark on a campaign to get discovered and remain relevant.

Since 2006, Marki has educated over 300,000 real estate professionals on how to utilize social media and technology to generate leads and build an online presence. There is no other place where consumers tell you their business in real time, and you have immediate access to them in order to send relevant content to help them solve their problems.

The Modern Real Estate Professionals Guide to Success reveals some of the numerous free and low-cost tools that Marki has utilized daily to add well over 4,800 contacts to her customer relationship management system annually. Social media is lead generation on steroids when you leverage it and create a comprehensive system.

Introduction

Marki Lemons Ryhal Provides Social Media and Technology Training to Real Estate Professionals

Twenty years ago, what I do today did not exist.

Lem's Bar-B-Q in Chicago is a family-owned business that has been feeding Chicagoans, tourists, and celebrities (including Aretha Franklin, Mike Tyson, Isaiah Thomas, and Monique) for sixty-three years. In 1999, a week before my twenty-ninth birthday, I received papers that I was being sued by an aunt for me to relinquish my ownership in Lem's Bar-B-Q and to hand over the trademark for Lem's that I solely owned. Being sued by one's family is heart-wrenching, and it cracks the foundation of the family. The underpinning of my family has never been repaired as a result of the lawsuit, due to the fact that it cost them money, as they had to settle with me. Hindsight is everything. The best thing that ever happened to my career was when my aunt sued me because it forced me to explore many other possibilities.

While going through the lawsuit, I decided I would enter into the world of residential lending because I needed a job that was flexible and yet would earn me an above average income. Within one year of entering the lending world, I was a top-producing mortgage broker and had generated over six figures in fees. I was promoted to a sales manager position, and I earned the coveted Certified Residential Mortgage Specialist designation from the National Association of Mortgage Brokers. I would go on from there to earn over fifty real estate-related licenses, certifications, and designations over the next sixteen years.

In 2002, I was reviewing my plan of action for 2003, and I realized that my numbers had me working around the clock. When I analyzed the numbers, I came to the conclusion that I could make the same amount of money if I left residential lending and utilized my real estate broker license. I would be able to close half the number of deals and work fewer hours. In 2003, I opened Homes2Sell, Inc., a Chicago-based discount real estate brokerage. Life was great as a Bronze level REALTOR®, and in 2004, I was among the top 10 percent of brokers in the city of Chicago.

Having a broker's license has afforded me several opportunities. Based on my past, I committed myself to become a lifelong learner. 2003 was only the beginning of my real estate sales career. I went on to serve on the board of directors for the third-largest local real estate board. I was also the Chair of the Chicago Association of REALTORS® Education Foundation, where as chairman, we provided $140,000 in complimentary real estate continuing education for our members.

I thought my world was coming to an end in 2006 because my grandfather died from Alzheimer-related issues, my mother died from a brain aneurysm, I suffered my third bout of pneumonia, I got married (a good thing) and then found out I was pregnant, but due to my age, I had a high-risk pregnancy. In October 2006, while traveling to Baltimore, I fainted on an airplane and was rushed to the hospital upon arrival. For the sake of my unborn child's health, it was recommended that I rest and take it easy. I had to make an extremely tough decision. Would I risk my health and that of my unborn child and go hard to save my business and real estate portfolio, or would I listen to my doctor's request? Financially, I lost everything while being blessed with my youngest son and the undivided loyalty of my husband.

I was actually at home on maternity leave when I decided to Google my name. My name came up less than ten times in that Google search. That was shocking to me because I had just read the 2006 Profiles of Buyers and Sellers from the National Association of REALTORS®. It had informed me that every single year since I had been licensed as a real estate broker, the percentage of buyers coming to the internet had increased. Today, 95 percent of all first-time home buyers start their search for a home on the internet, and 67 percent of them are likely to do business with the first person they come in contact with.

My mentor, Mr. Frank Williams, made the recommendation that I become a licensed real estate instructor, as it would provide me with the ability to connect with licensed individuals consistently. As I was rebuilding my business, I decided to focus on real estate education. Within three years of becoming a licensed instructor, I was speaking on a national level for organizations like the National Association of REALTORS® and REBAC. That national exposure afforded me the opportunity to launch the Accredited Distressed Property Representative designation that educated over five thousand REALTORS® on foreclosures and short sales.

Even though foreclosure education opened the doors to several new opportunities, I had fallen back in love with marketing. I have an MBA degree in marketing, but the marketing I was exploring was all new and had only been around for a few years, and that was social media marketing. Social media marketing was natural to me, as I applied online concepts to what I was already doing offline. 2012 was a defining moment for me, as I made yet another career move, and that was to focus on social media education for real estate. Social media has taken me into classrooms internationally. I've partnered with the biggest names in real estate, like the National Association of REALTORS®, Homes.com, Matterport, CHASE, Chicago Title, BMO Harris, and Goldman Sachs 10,000 Small Businesses, to name a few. We provided social media seminars and continuing education courses for licensed individuals in three formats, face-to-face, live-streaming video, and in a webinar format.

There used to be a saying: "American Express, don't leave home without it." What's the one thing that you don't leave home without today? It's your mobile device. Today, everything has a mobile app.

Social media is the one place that people will tell you all of their business in real time. Are you listening?

There are two kinds of agents:
1) those who do the
same non-productive things
over and over and 2) those
who quickly adapt to a
fast-changing environment.
Which agent are you?
#RealEstate
#SuccessfulAgents

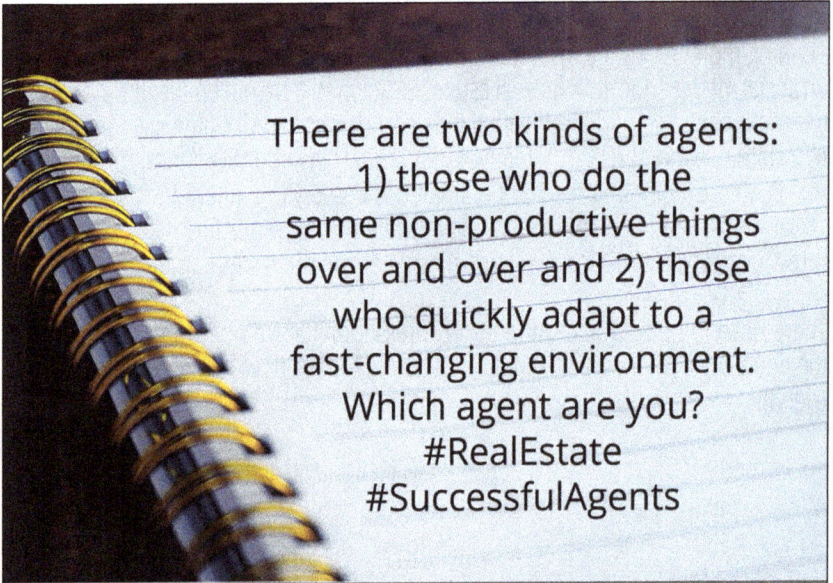

Marki Lemons Ryhal
http://aha.pub/RealEstateGuide

Share the AHA messages from this book socially by going to
http://aha.pub/RealEstateGuide.

Section I

Who Are the Real Estate Professionals of Today?

In the world of real estate, we have disrupters, or new business models, that come to the market every single day. In order to adjust, today's real estate professionals have to embrace the fact that change is constant, because there's going to be something different every single day, and it means that the way we do business today may not be as efficient tomorrow.

Today's agents acknowledge the fact that they're entrepreneurs and they treat their real estate career like a business. Thus, it is their responsibility as business owners to keep up with any changes in their industry in order to remain relevant and successful. The agents who succeed are those who are able to change quickly in a fast-changing environment.

Watch this video:
http://aha.pub/RealEstateGuideS1

1

There are two kinds of agents: 1) those who do the same non-productive things over and over and 2) those who quickly adapt to a fast-changing environment. Which agent are you? #RealEstate #SuccessfulAgents

_____

_____

_____

2

Today's agents embrace change as constant and that there is going to be something different every single day. Keeping up with change by changing strategies and tactics leads to a sustainable #RealEstate business. #SuccessfulAgents

_____

_____

_____

3

Today's agents deliberately know their environment, continually educate themselves about it, and figure out how to prospect for new business. Do you? #RealEstate #SuccessfulAgents

---

4

Like anything else in life, if you're going to be an agent, there's no easy money. #RealEstate is a business, so you need to treat it like one if you want to succeed. #SuccessfulAgents

---

5

Agents of today know that they're independent contractors and entrepreneurs and that they're responsible for their own success.
#RealEstate #SuccessfulAgents

_____

_____

_____

6

No business requires sitting in the office all the time, especially #RealEstate! Today's agents meet plenty of people offline, attend networking events, and gather as many business contacts as possible to generate more leads. #SuccessfulAgents

_____

_____

_____

7

If you're aiming for millions of dollars, don't just sit and wait for your broker to give you leads. Today's agents go out and generate leads. #RealEstate #SuccessfulAgents

_____

_____

_____

8

There is no instant success in #RealEstate. Today's agents start months in advance to earn market share. How much time do you put into planning your business? #SuccessfulAgents

_____

_____

_____

9

Today's agents utilize modern technology to get in touch with their prospects and close business. Are you leveraging technology in your #RealEstate business? #SuccessfulAgents

_____

_____

_____

10

Today's agents know how to easily adapt to technology and new business models that come to the market every single day. Are you able to embrace technology when it comes? #RealEstate #SuccessfulAgents

_____

_____

_____

11

Today's agents make use of technology to control and automate processes in their #RealEstate business because it makes things more efficient. How much control do you have over your business? #SuccessfulAgents

_____

_____

_____

12

Technology is unstoppable from dominating industries, including #RealEstate. As an agent in today's world, what are you doing to get the most out of modern technology? #SuccessfulAgents

_____

_____

_____

13

Technology will never replace an agent. However, an agent with technology will replace an agent without technology. #RealEstate #SuccessfulAgents

_____

_____

_____

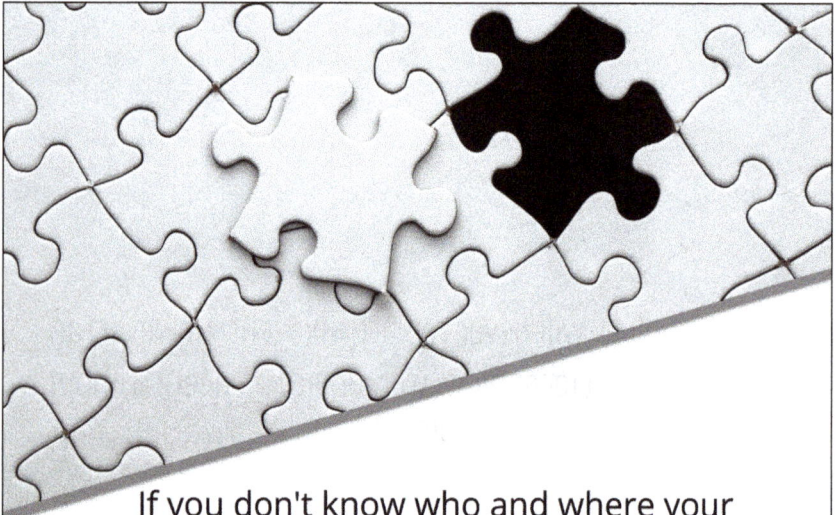

If you don't know who and where your prospects are, then you don't have clients. If you don't have clients, you don't have a business.
#KnowYourClients #SuccessfulAgents

Marki Lemons Ryhal
http://aha.pub/RealEstateGuide

Share the AHA messages from this book socially by going to
http://aha.pub/RealEstateGuide.

Section II

Who Are Your Prospects and Where Can You Find Them?

As a real estate agent, you need to know who and where your prospects are.

There are two main types of real estate clients: the buyer and the seller. Buyers and sellers are different customers. Buyers are on the internet looking at their possibilities in real time, while sellers engage with direct mail campaigns followed up with online research. Having an understanding of your target audience and deciding if you want to be a buyer's agent or a listings agent will allow you to operate a more efficient real estate business.

Successful agents also have a community that they dominate and serve. Choosing a community that embraces and supports you is a good starting point for any agent.

Watch this video:
http://aha.pub/RealEstateGuideS2

14

There are around 20 percent of agents who can easily tell you exactly where, for what, and whom they do their #RealEstate business. Are you part of that 20 percent? #KnowYourClients #SuccessfulAgents http://bit.ly/2Y42OmB

_____

_____

_____

15

There are five important things #SuccessfulAgents know: 1) the area they serve, 2) the businesses in that area, 3) the prospects in that area, 4) the prospect's desire, and 5) the information they seek. Do you? #KnowYourClients

_____

_____

_____

16

Focusing on a niche allows agents to easily identify and reach their prospects, so they can gain expertise to better serve them. #KnowYourClients #SuccessfulAgents

_____

_____

_____

17

The agents who make the most money are those who have a specific niche they serve and know the best way to serve the prospects in that niche. #KnowYourClients #SuccessfulAgents

_____

_____

_____

18

What matters most in #RealEstate is who you know and how you are known. It just does not work when agents try to service everyone. Find your niche! #KnowYourClients #SuccessfulAgents

_____

_____

_____

19

Simply put, there are two primary types of #RealEstate clients: 1) the buyer and 2) the seller. Agents who know who their clients are provide better service than those who serve everyone. #KnowYourClients #SuccessfulAgents

_____

_____

20

Buyers are on the internet receiving a lot of the information they need in real time, while sellers still want to receive content online and offline. #SuccessfulAgents know whom they represent in the market. Do you know? #KnowYourClients

_____

_____

_____

21

Helping people is great, but don't make yourself a "Master of the Universe" in the process. You'll burn yourself out, cripple people, and end up with people who resent you. #KnowYourClients #SuccessfulAgents

_____

_____

_____

22

When you identify your audience, it's easier to develop content and an approach in which you're going to reach out to them. Do you know who your audience is? #KnowYourClients #SuccessfulAgents

---

23

67 percent of online #RealEstate searches start with location. That's why it's important for agents to carefully establish their location. #KnowYourClients #SuccessfulAgents

---

24

Before agents start their #RealEstate business, they should first know the community they want to dominate. Have you found the community you'll serve? #KnowYourClients #SuccessfulAgents

_____

_____

_____

25

Pick a community that is willing to embrace you. Understand the language and the ins and outs of the community. #KnowYourClients #SuccessfulAgents

_____

_____

_____

26

There are three things that new agents should consider when picking a community: 1) it has a high rate of sale, 2) it's at their desired price point, and 3) it has the lowest barriers to entry. #KnowYourClients #SuccessfulAgents

_____

_____

27

If you aim to get a paycheck quicker, find a community
with the fastest rate of sell, at the highest price
point, and with the fewest barriers to entry. Agents
who go beyond the average earn above average.
#KnowYourClients #SuccessfulAgents

_____

_____

_____

28

#SuccessfulAgents are wise in targeting a community.
Carefully look at the numbers, make a side-by-side
comparison, and choose a community that is willing to
embrace you and help you succeed. #KnowYourClients

_____

_____

_____

29

#SuccessfulAgents know the people living in the community, including their average household income, family size and structure, and what things they do on a weekend. #KnowYourClients

---

30

Be an active member of the chamber of commerce in your area. Chances are, people are going to know, like, and trust you as a result of your volunteer efforts. #KnowYourClients #SuccessfulAgents

---

31

Being involved in the local community plays a big part for agents who are just getting started in the #RealEstate business. Are you involved in your local community? #KnowYourClients #SuccessfulAgents

_____

_____

_____

32

Many agents do not see the value of volunteering and how it will actually put them in roles that will open doors they could not have opened by themselves. How involved are you in your community? #KnowYourClients #SuccessfulAgents

_____

_____

33

Utilize the Multiple Listing Service because it's one of the best places where agents can find their prospects. How often do you use the MLS? #KnowYourClients #SuccessfulAgents

_____

_____

_____

34

If you don't know who and where your prospects are, then you don't have clients. If you don't have clients, you don't have a business. #KnowYourClients #SuccessfulAgents

_____

_____

_____

There are transactions where we don't meet people face to face, but that does not mean that we shouldn't use an online tool for face-to-face meetings.
#SuccessfulAgents

Marki Lemons Ryhal
http://aha.pub/RealEstateGuide

Share the AHA messages from this book socially by going to
http://aha.pub/RealEstateGuide.

Section III

The Role of Human Touch and Social Media in Your Real Estate Business

Social media and technology play a huge part in the real estate industry. There are technology components included in every step of the real estate transaction. Agents need to understand how utilizing social media and technology every day can help them become more efficient.

Watch this video:
http://aha.pub/RealEstateGuideS3

35

Modern agents need to realize that human touch and social media play a significant role in their #RealEstate business. Do you make use of both elements? #SuccessfulAgents

_____

_____

_____

36

If you only have online connections, you have a 1-in-50 chance of converting them into a client. If you meet them face to face, your chances shift to 1 in 6. #SuccessfulAgents

_____

_____

_____

37

Meet as many people as possible offline so you'll cultivate more potential leads. Having the human touch will help you connect with them. #SuccessfulAgents

_____

_____

_____

38

Agents need to leverage the face-to-face interaction they have with people they've met by using social media to further generate trust and build the relationship. #SuccessfulAgents

---

39

When networking, you have to be up to speed with technology and use it, but you also need to make sure you understand and touch humans. #SuccessfulAgents

---

40

There are transactions where we don't meet people face to face, but that does not mean that we shouldn't use an online tool for face-to-face meetings. #SuccessfulAgents

_____

_____

_____

41

Being up to speed with technology does not mean you eliminate meeting people face to face. #SuccessfulAgents leverage personal meetings with technology. Do you?

_____

_____

_____

42

Take your online relationships offline so you have a substantially higher conversion rate because you meet people face to face. #SuccessfulAgents

_____

_____

_____

43

Networking with the enhancement of technology will allow you to supercharge your businesses and get more leads. #SuccessfulAgents

_____

_____

_____

Being "online" means allowing yourself to be seen by others and you seeing them. This gives you ideas of who may become a customer tomorrow who's not a customer today. Are you "online"? #SocialMediaTips #SuccessfulAgents

Marki Lemons Ryhal
http://aha.pub/RealEstateGuide

Share the AHA messages from this book socially by going to
http://aha.pub/RealEstateGuide.

Section IV

Social Media Best Practices for Real Estate Professionals

Social media has become one of the favorite pastimes for people all over the world. Many people start their day by going to their social media accounts and scrolling through their feeds. Agents need to take advantage of social media as a means to get visibility for and from their potential clients.

As an agent, you need to listen to a consumer's needs and wants in real time. Come up with fresh ideas and tactics to close any deal as quickly as possible. Social media is a great way to be known for providing value, improving lives, and helping people solve their problems and achieve their goals.

Watch this video:
http://aha.pub/RealEstateGuideS4

44

Prospects will tell you their needs in real time through social media. #SuccessfulAgents listen and try to understand how those needs can be fulfilled, and they then present solutions. #SocialMediaTips http://bit.ly/2SECcml

_____

_____

_____

45

Do you know how to listen to your prospects on social media? #SuccessfulAgents start by searching for keywords, hashtags, and location-based check-ins to see if they can help people with their needs. #SocialMediaTips

_____

_____

46

Take advantage of the fact that most people today check their social media accounts as soon as they wake up in the morning. #SocialMediaTips #SuccessfulAgents

_____

_____

_____

47

Social media is often checked faster than email. People have a plethora of opportunities to keep their eyes on you, your brand, and your #RealEstate business. Is your online identity aligned with your true self? #SocialMediaTips #SuccessfulAgents

_____

_____

48

Find a balance between who you are as an agent and what people want to see on social media. #SocialMediaTips #SuccessfulAgents

_____

_____

_____

49

When you engage with people online, don't publicly discuss sensitive topics such as politics and religion. Remember, you're in the business to make money, so avoid offending and alienating anyone. #SocialMediaTips #SuccessfulAgents

_____

_____

50

Making an impact on social media is not about showing how many houses you've sold, it's about giving information that's relevant and impactful to consumers in your market. #SocialMediaTips #SuccessfulAgents http://bit.ly/2ydo3D7

_____

_____

_____

51

#SuccessfulAgents strive to be known for providing value and mentorship and improving lives. Leverage social media to do this seamlessly and sustainably. #SocialMediaTips

_____

_____

52

People want to see the authentic, transparent version of you. #SuccessfulAgents know that clients don't want to hear scripts because they feel like you're selling them. Are you an authentic agent? #SocialMediaTips

---

53

The business of #RealEstate is about making connections. To keep a connection, you have to be your true authentic self online and present that same personality offline. #SocialMediaTips #SuccessfulAgents

---

54

Social media is not about being a certain personality or playing a role—it's about having a tool for us to be ourselves and highlight what makes us unique.
#SocialMediaTips #SuccessfulAgents

_____

_____

_____

55

The biggest challenge #RealEstate professionals face in social selling is the belief that we have to be a certain persona to succeed. Nothing beats a person who's authentic and true both online and offline.
#SocialMediaTips #SuccessfulAgents

_____

_____

56

Whether you are seen online or offline by your clients, you need to be authentic. Be the same person as you are online. Otherwise, people will disconnect from you and not trust you. #SocialMediaTips #SuccessfulAgents

_____

_____

_____

57

Many people today are attached to their mobile devices. #SuccessfulAgents ensure that they're visible online at all times. Have you posted something good today? #RealEstateBusiness. #SocialMediaTips

_____

_____

_____

58

As business people, we need to be online, but then, we also need to talk to consumers the way they search in order for us to be found. #SocialMediaTips #SuccessfulAgents

_____

_____

_____

59

Being "online" means allowing yourself to be seen by others and you seeing them. This gives you ideas of who may become a customer tomorrow who's not a customer today. Are you "online"? #SocialMediaTips #SuccessfulAgents

_____

_____

_____

60

Let your existence be made known. #SuccessfulAgents stay relevant by continuously feeding their social media stories every day. #SocialMediaTips

_____

_____

_____

61

Generate leads by using a Call to Action (CTA). Capture people by allowing them to subscribe on your landing page. Have you thought of a CTA for today? #SocialMediaTips #SuccessfulAgents

_____

_____

_____

62

Mobile business cards are a way to give out your information to people and make it easy for them to download your contact information. We'll no longer have to worry about running out of cards. #SocialMediaTips #SuccessfulAgents

_____

_____

_____

63

The first step to building a #RealEstate business is to let people know that you are in the business. How many calls, texts, emails, or mobile business cards have you sent out today? #SocialMediaTips #SuccessfulAgents

_____

_____

_____

64

A social media strategy that works right now might fail in the future. To ensure continuous success, make sure you have your contacts in a Customer Relationship Management System. #SocialMediaTips #SuccessfulAgents

_____

_____

65

Facebook is not just a tool that generates leads, it's an accelerator. When we put the right systems in place and maximize Facebook, it will help grow our business. Are you leveraging Facebook? #SocialMediaTips #SuccessfulAgents

_____

_____

_____

66

Post on a regular basis, but do not always post about #RealEstate. Use the 80/20 ratio: 80% personal content and 20% business. #SocialMediaTips #SuccessfulAgents

_____

_____

_____

67

Post something relevant every 24 hours on your social media channels to give prospects a gentle reminder of how the things you do every single day can benefit them. #SocialMediaTips #SuccessfulAgents

_____

_____

_____

68

Stories disappear in 24 hours, so get into the habit of creating vertical content every single day if you want to be seen in the story feed and not have to pay for that exposure. #SocialMediaTips #SuccessfulAgents

_____

_____

_____

69

Consider IGTV because it's being prioritized.
Instagram's algorithm puts more IGTV videos into
people's feeds, which means more engagement.
#SocialMediaTips #SuccessfulAgents

_____

_____

_____

70

Facebook Live allows agents to broadcast to the largest
audience in the world with just a camera and Wi-Fi.
It lets you connect with consumers, customers,
and clients. Are you using Facebook Live?
#SocialMediaTips #SuccessfulAgents

_____

_____

71

Commit to fifteen minutes a day to connect with people and build relationships. Make use of the Live features of Facebook and Instagram to get your momentum going and build up from there. #SocialMediaTips #SuccessfulAgents

_____

_____

_____

72

Live streaming video is screen-to-screen selling. It's the next-best thing to meeting someone in person. #SocialMediaTips #SuccessfulAgents

_____

_____

_____

73

You can utilize today's technological tools to generate more real estate leads, but be aware that these tools can become obsolete tomorrow. #SuccessfulAgents are up to date with tech. Are you? #SocialMediaTips

_____

_____

_____

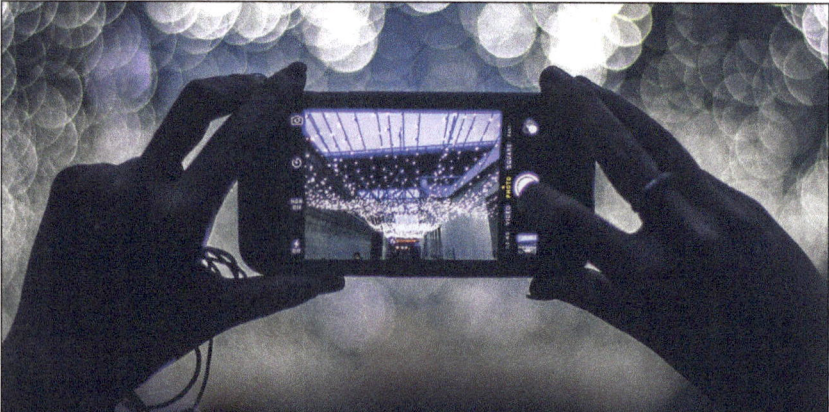

They used to say a picture is worth a thousand words. Well, today, one minute of video content is worth 1.8 million words. Are you creating one-minute videos? #VisualContent #SuccessfulAgents http://bit.ly/2JUs32b

Marki Lemons Ryhal
http://aha.pub/RealEstateGuide

Share the AHA messages from this book socially by going to
http://aha.pub/RealEstateGuide.

Section V

If a Picture Is Worth a Thousand Words . . .
Videos Are Worth Even More

Photos and videos play a huge role in marketing homes today. Both lead to more showings, awareness, and success.

The majority of home buyers start their searches online. Pictures and videos are what make the quickest and largest impression on buyers. Although they will not instantly sell your home, they attract buyers to you. You need to produce quality photos and videos so they market you well on the internet, social media, and MLS!

As an agent, you need to learn how to leverage photos and videos on social media. You need to talk to the community you serve constantly.

Watch this video:
http://aha.pub/RealEstateGuideS5

74

There are thousands of platforms where agents can post photos and videos, but those who succeed know how to get their photos and videos to talk to people. #VisualContent #SuccessfulAgents http://bit.ly/2YgO8MI

_____

_____

_____

75

Make your content more engaging by accompanying it with catchy photos and/or videos about what problem you can solve on someone's behalf.
#VisualContent #SuccessfulAgents

_____

_____

_____

76

Nowadays, not only do you need an image, but you also need to step up your visual game, catching your audience's eye as they scroll by.
#VisualContent #SuccessfulAgents

_____

_____

_____

77

#SuccessfulAgents capture and share photos of the chosen community that they want to dominate. Have you taken one picture today and shared it? #VisualContent

_____

_____

_____

78

Never let your device's power get low, because great memories can happen at any moment. Be ready to capture them. #VisualContent #SuccessfulAgents

_____

_____

_____

79

In producing photos, go beyond what's inside the property. Take pictures that will simulate a complete experience for prospective buyers. #VisualContent #SuccessfulAgents

_____

_____

_____

80

Posting photos on #RealEstate platforms is only one step. Creating quality photos is another thing. Are you nailing it? #VisualContent #SuccessfulAgents

_____

_____

_____

81

Agents who want to get the absolute best should also produce the best. Invest in the best cameras to capture the best photos. #VisualContent #SuccessfulAgents

_____

_____

_____

82

Today's cameras have amazing technological features that are helpful for agents, such as wide angle mode and low light mode. What features are you taking advantage of now? #VisualContent #SuccessfulAgents

_____

_____

_____

83

#SuccessfulAgents invest in a camera, wipe its lenses, and produce pictures that paint a thousand words. Do you make all your photos count? #VisualContent

_____

_____

_____

84

Aside from regularly cleaning the camera's lenses, #SuccessfulAgents learn how to get the right angle, surroundings, and elements to focus on. Do you highlight the unique? #VisualContent

_____

_____

_____

85

Sometimes, the secret behind producing quality #RealEstate photos is just cleaning the camera lens. Are you cleaning your lens before taking shots? #VisualContent #SuccessfulAgents

_____

_____

_____

86

If you want to be a #SuccessfulAgent today, invest in excellent vertical photos that you can post on your social media stories every 24 hours. #VisualContent

_____

_____

_____

87

In order to make unforgettable #VisualContent, you have to know what kind of content your target audience responds to, and then create it. Always remember that the goal is to bring value and make an emotional impact. #SuccessfulAgents

---

88

There are two forms of video content to connect with your audience: 1) a personal video that will let you engage with people by letting them know you and 2) a lead generation video where you add a CTA to a landing page. #VisualContent #SuccessfulAgents

_____

_____

_____

89

#SuccessfulAgents understand how a live video gets them as close to meeting people personally as possible. When was the last time you created a livestream? #VisualContent

_____

_____

_____

90

Video content doesn't have to be the lesser version of a face-to-face conversation. We have to get comfortable with it by forcing ourselves to do it until it becomes a habit. #VisualContent #SuccessfulAgents

_____

_____

_____

91

When producing videos, don't do a lot of editing, because people still want to see the true and authentic version of you. #VisualContent #SuccessfulAgents

_____

_____

_____

92

Cutting videos down to roughly a minute can let you dominate every platform. Make all sixty seconds count.
#VisualContent #SuccessfulAgents

_____

_____

_____

93

To get ahead using social media, video content is non-negotiable. While professional video is popular, remember that at the core, your videos need to serve the needs of your audience. #VisualContent #SuccessfulAgents

_____

_____

_____

94

Agents who can create at least sixty seconds of video every single day gain more connections than those who don't. #VisualContent #SuccessfulAgents

_____

_____

_____

95

They used to say a picture is worth a thousand words. Well, today, one minute of video content is worth 1.8 million words. Are you creating one-minute videos? #VisualContent #SuccessfulAgents http://bit.ly/2JUs32b

_____

_____

_____

As an agent, you're the repository of so much information and #Value. You cannot be replaced by a computer. Don't worry, start sharing valuable content! #SuccessfulAgents #CreateValue

Marki Lemons Ryhal
http://aha.pub/RealEstateGuide

Share the AHA messages from this book socially by going to
http://aha.pub/RealEstateGuide.

Section VI

Why Creating Valuable Content Is Important for Your Real Estate Business

Have you ever heard the phrase, "Content is king?" Yes, it's true. Behind every successful business or brand is a wealth of relevant and valuable content that fuels their digital marketing campaigns and connects with their customers.

Great content helps you build trust with your target audience. If people find your content engaging, valuable, and educational, they will start to develop a favorable opinion about your brand and see you as a thought leader in the industry.

Watch this video:
http://aha.pub/RealEstateGuideS6

96

Agents who always think about leveraging will most likely succeed. In today's world, leveraging starts with making good, valuable content. What's your latest content about? #SuccessfulAgents #CreateValue

_____

_____

_____

97

In #RealEstate, we're not just collecting names, we're providing valuable information in exchange for attention, which is determined by how personalized our message is. How personalized is your content? #SuccessfulAgents #CreateValue

_____

_____

98

The relevance and authenticity of your content is how people make the connection with you, and it makes them want to buy from you. How relevant and authentic is the content you're posting?
#SuccessfulAgents #CreateValue

_____

_____

_____

99

If you're constantly posting content that 1) just sells to people, 2) doesn't pique their interest, and 3) doesn't authentically show who you are, it won't make an impact. What content are you posting?
#SuccessfulAgents #CreateValue

_____

_____

100

When it comes to contacting people, it starts with the initial numbers. The power is your closing ratio and the quality of the interactions you have. #SuccessfulAgents #CreateValue

_____

_____

_____

101

What truly marks the success of your content isn't how many people viewed it, it's about how many actually engaged with it. Make sure your content has value! #SuccessfulAgents #CreateValue

---

102

A key technique to driving success as an agent is to be the resource of information that clients crave. Offer value, tips, and insights that show your expertise. #SuccessfulAgents #CreateValue

103

You don't need the perfect strategy or the perfect content to get started with social media. Begin with what you have, and make a habit of creating and sharing content daily. #SuccessfulAgents #CreateValue

_____

_____

_____

104

Create content for the people you want to attract and bring you new business. Interview experts or speak to people in your area of influence, just be sure to keep the camera rolling! #SuccessfulAgents #CreateValue

_____

_____

_____

105

To take advantage of your slower times, create bulk content during slow days and spread that content throughout the week to efficiently manage your #RealEstate social media accounts. #SuccessfulAgents #CreateValue

_____

_____

106

#SuccessfulAgents create content that can be used on multiple platforms and repurposed. Are you investing in quality repurposable content? #CreateValue

_____

_____

_____

107

When we are doing our work, meeting and talking with people, many nuggets and pieces of information are thrown at us. We need to take that content and share it with the world because it has value.
#SuccessfulAgents #CreateValue

_____

_____

_____

108

To become an influential agent, invest on curating content from past clients, your local community, and trade associations. #SuccessfulAgents #CreateValue

_____

_____

_____

109

Your local, state, and the National Association of REALTORS are producing content. #SuccessfulAgents optimize this content to their advantage. Do you? #CreateValue

_____

_____

_____

110

Be involved in the local community and think of user-generated content that you can use to leverage your #RealEstate business. #SuccessfulAgents #CreateValue

_____

_____

_____

111

As an agent, you're the repository of so much information and #Value. You cannot be replaced by a computer. Don't worry, start sharing valuable content! #SuccessfulAgents #CreateValue

_____

_____

_____

#SuccessfulAgents never underestimate the power of #Referrals. If done right, you can earn as much money from referrals as you can from selling #RealEstate.

Revenue

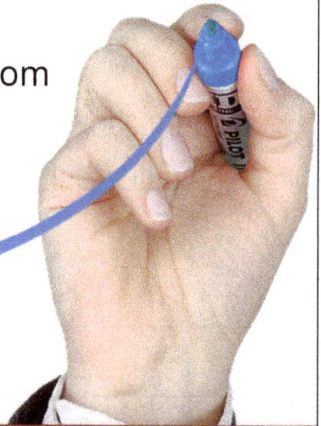

Marki Lemons Ryhal
http://aha.pub/RealEstateGuide

Share the AHA messages from this book socially by going to
http://aha.pub/RealEstateGuide.

Section VII

The Power of Referrals

Referrals are a vital component of the real estate business. It is a higher converting revenue system that allows you to get to the first stage of the sales process. From there, you begin to develop a client courtship in order to win a new client and make the sale.

The most interesting thing about referrals is that it goes both ways—referring clients to others, as well as receiving referrals—and the better you are at being a referrer, the better referrals you will attract.

Watch this video:
http://aha.pub/RealEstateGuideS7

112

#SuccessfulAgents never underestimate the power of #Referrals. If done right, you can earn as much money from referrals as you can from selling #RealEstate.

_____

_____

_____

113

Once you are a licensed real estate agent and you make a #Referral, there is a percentage of that transaction that you can receive. #SuccessfulAgents

_____

_____

_____

114

Because a REALTOR® is an entrepreneur, they create a business plan to follow which helps them plan for their #RealEstate success. #SuccessfulRealtors

_____

_____

_____

115

As an agent, you need to leverage your face-to-face interaction. Give people something of value and make sure you ask for #Referrals. #SuccessfulAgents

_____

_____

_____

116

When you do ask for #Referrals, you need to have an effective follow-up strategy in place to ensure that all parties receive value. #SuccessfulAgents

_____

_____

_____

117

Referrers are like your personal ambassadors. They are the ones who have the courage to speak highly of you and refer you willingly. Do you have ambassadors? #Referrals #SuccessfulAgents

_____

_____

_____

118

Ambassadors don't just show up on their own, we have to nurture them by giving value and caring about them because that bleeds into the questions we ask, the things we say, and the way we treat them.
#Referrals #SuccessfulAgents

_____

_____

_____

119

Mobilize your army of personal ambassadors because if you get someone who likes you together with someone else who likes you, they will both love you.
#Referrals #SuccessfulAgents

_____

_____

_____

120

Ambassadors are people who can help a #RealEstate business succeed. The better you get at being an ambassador, the better ambassadors you'll attract to yourself. #Referrals #SuccessfulAgents

_____

_____

_____

121

The moment you try to be all things to all people, you reduce the likelihood of receiving #Referrals because people do not know who to refer to you. #SuccessfulAgents

_____

_____

_____

122

If you only want to do listings or represent the seller, do so. Make sure sure you don't turn away buyers but refer them instead to the best buyer agent you know who is going to close the deal. #Referrals #SuccessfulAgents

_____

_____

_____

123

#SuccessfulAgents leverage referrals in their #RealEstate business. If you can't handle a client, referring them to someone better will ultimately bring great returns. #Referrals

_____

_____

_____

124

When you cannot help a prospect, give them other options by referring them to those you know can help them succeed. #Referrals #SuccessfulAgents

_____

_____

_____

125

One way to leverage is through #Referrals. If you can't handle that business, refer it to a person who's better than you, get a referral fee, and focus on the business that you have. #SuccessfulAgents

_____

_____

_____

126

Serving a consumer may sometimes mean turning them away or recommending somebody else. Doing this politely results in gaining trust of prospects and receiving #Referrals from them. #SuccessfulAgents

_____

_____

_____

What truly separates agents is the
level of service they
give their clients. To fetch the
commission we want, we
have to deliver value that sets us
apart and makes us
different from everyone else.
#SuccessfulAgents

Marki Lemons Ryhal
http://aha.pub/RealEstateGuide

Share the AHA messages from this book socially by going to
http://aha.pub/RealEstateGuide.

Section VIII

Key Elements of Success in the World of Real Estate

There is no shortcut to success in real estate. It takes a lot of hard work and effort to start and build a profitable and successful real estate business. Agents need to ensure that everything they do is relevant and contributes to helping them reach the next level.

It's important for agents to remember that they should come from a place of helping to solve problems. Be where your prospects are, and use the best and latest iterations of technology to leverage everything you do. Think outside the box, do what no one else is doing, stand out from the crowd, and succeed.

Watch this video:
http://aha.pub/RealEstateGuideS8

127

Successful agents surround themselves with people who are substantially better than they are. Are you surrounding yourself with more #SuccessfulAgents?

_____

_____

_____

128

Many agents haven't stopped to really think who their influencers are. Think about the whole professional ecosystem working in real estate and build relationships with the right influencers. #SuccessfulAgents

_____

_____

_____

129

You don't have to be the smartest agent. You just need to continually think about and act on growing your #RealEstate business. #SuccessfulAgents

_____

_____

_____

130

There's something new with social media and technology every day. To be a #SuccessfulAgent, you need to become a lifelong learner.

_____

_____

_____

131

Make sure everything you do has a strategy behind it, and be consistent. The strategy that works is the one that meets the numbers outlined in your business plan. #SuccessfulAgents

_____

_____

_____

132

You can predict your #RealEstate success by being intentional in creating it. Schedule daily, weekly, and monthly activities for you to succeed. #SuccessfulAgents

_____

_____

_____

133

Hone who you are, be comfortable in your own skin, and really highlight who that is online. #SuccessfulAgents

_____

_____

_____

134

You need to be the same person offline as you are online. You've got to be your true authentic self, and you have to have that same personality offline or else people will disconnect from you. #SuccessfulAgents

_____

_____

_____

135

Be an honest and transparent agent. Know who you are, who is in your market, and the different ways you could serve them. #SuccessfulAgents

---

136

#SuccessfulAgents make timely follow-ups and know how to communicate with prospects in their preferred communication style.

137

Agents who position themselves as advisors and add value to other people's lives can't be replaced easily. How are you positioning yourself in your #RealEstate business? #SuccessfulAgents

_____

_____

_____

138

Running a #RealEstate business requires intention and purpose. Show up well-dressed, interact with people, and have the confidence to ask for the business. #SuccessfulAgents

_____

_____

_____

139

People will always remember how you made them feel, so you need to make them feel good. Always teach them something they did not know before they met you. #SuccessfulAgents

_____

_____

_____

140

What truly separates agents is the level of service they give their clients. To fetch the commission we want, we have to deliver value that sets us apart and makes us different from everyone else. #SuccessfulAgents

_____

_____

_____

Appendix

In reviewing this book, I realized there's much more content I can share with you. This appendix includes links to an extended video and blog post on each of the sections of the book.

Please send an email to info@markilemons.com if you wish to receive a PDF copy with the clickable links listed below.

Section I — Who Are the Realtors of Today?
Marki Lemons Ryhal summarizing the section: http://aha.pub/RealEstateGuideS1
Social Selling Made Simple video: https://youtu.be/UvXf2zg08t0
Blog post: https://markilemons.com/goal-setting-strategies/

Section II — Who Are Your Prospects and Where Can You Find Them?
Marki Lemons Ryhal summarizing the section: http://aha.pub/RealEstateGuideS2
Social Selling Made Simple video: https://youtu.be/h0S6WHYfjpU
Blog post: https://markilemons.com/how-to-leverage-mls-data-to-boost-your-real-estate-business-w-carrie-little/

Section III — The Role of Human Touch and Social Media in Your Real Estate Business
Marki Lemons Ryhal summarizing the section: http://aha.pub/RealEstateGuideS3
Social Selling Made Simple video: https://youtu.be/wbLhc61gpyl
Blog post: https://markilemons.com/how-to-build-a-solid-foundation-for-your-real-estate-business-w-candy-miles-crocker/

Section IV — Social Media Best Practices for Realtors
Marki Lemons Ryhal summarizing the section: http://aha.pub/RealEstateGuideS4
Social Selling Made Simple video: https://youtu.be/UuQUU9EA4nA
Blog post: https://markilemons.com/how-to-enhance-real-estate-with-technology-w-annette-anthony/

Section V — If a Picture Is Worth a Thousand Words . . . Videos Are Worth Even More

Marki Lemons Ryhal summarizing the section: http://aha.pub/RealEstateGuideS5
Social Selling Made Simple video: https://youtu.be/UeVYAcG-1vY
Blog post: https://markilemons.com/video-is-here-to-stay-so-start-using-it-now/

Section VI — Why Creating Valuable Content Is Important for Your Real Estate Business

Marki Lemons Ryhal summarizing the section: http://aha.pub/RealEstateGuideS6
Social Selling Made Simple video: https://youtu.be/levJjUs9f4c
Blog post: https://markilemons.com/how-to-attract-clients-build-a-local-following-generate-agent-referrals-on-instagram-w-dustin-brohm/

Section VII — The Power of Referrals

Marki Lemons Ryhal summarizing the section: http://aha.pub/RealEstateGuideS7
Social Selling Made Simple video: https://youtu.be/Zx9-aQyHkUk
Blog post: https://markilemons.com/how-to-find-mobilize-and-train-an-army-of-personal-ambassadors-w-michael-maher/

Section VIII — Key Elements of Success in the World of Real Estate

Marki Lemons Ryhal summarizing the section: http://aha.pub/RealEstateGuideS8
Social Selling Made Simple video: https://youtu.be/4nKccIPH8sE
Blog post: https://markilemons.com/how-to-successfully-create-a-process-for-sales-lead-follow-up-and-conversion-w-wes-schaeffer/

About the Author

Marki Lemons Ryhal is a Licensed Managing Broker, REALTOR, avid volunteer, and major donor. She is dedicated to all things real estate. With over twenty-five years of marketing experience, Marki has taught over 300,000 real estate professionals how to earn up to a 2,682 percent return on their marketing dollars. As a REALTOR, Marki has earned several sales awards, the REALTOR Achievement Award, and The President's Award from the Chicago Association of REALTORS. She is also a six-time REALTOR Conference and Expo-featured attendee, one of 100 speakers selected to speak six times at the REALTOR Conference and Expo, and an Inman closing keynote speaker.

By consistently offering sound industry analysis and professional guidance, Marki's expertise has been featured in *Forbes, The Washington Post*, Homes.com, and *REALTOR* magazine. She holds a bachelor of science in management from Chicago State University, a master's in business administration from Saint Xavier University, and over fifty real-estate-related licenses, certifications, and designations.

THiNKaha has created AHAthat for you to share content from this book.

- ⮑ Share each AHA message socially:
  http://aha.pub/RealEstateGuide

- ⮑ Share additional content: **https://AHAthat.com**

- ⮑ Info on authoring: **https://AHAthat.com/Author**

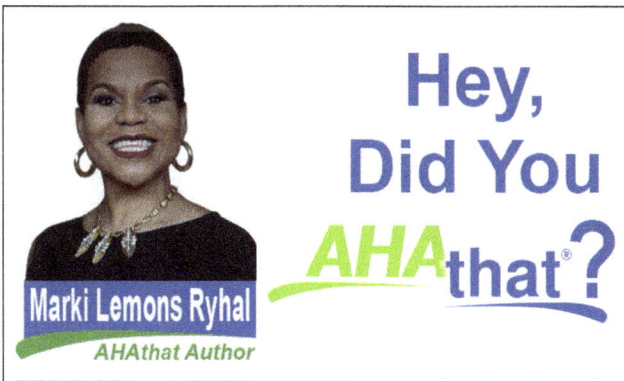

www.ingramcontent.com/pod-product-compliance
Lightning Source LLC
Chambersburg PA
CBHW071204200326
41519CB00018B/5356